# O'regan press

Library of Congress Cataloging-in-Publication Data is available on file.
First printing

Hardcover ISBN: 978-09908774-1-7
Softcover ISBN: 978-09908774-0-0

Printed in Canada

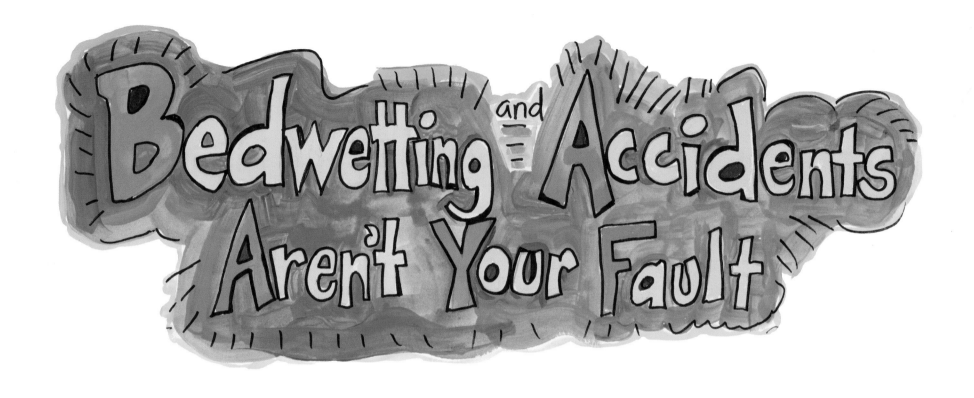

Written by

**Steve Hodges, M.D., & Suzanne Schlosberg**

Illustrated by

**Cristina Acosta**

This book is dedicated to

Stella Grace, Abigail,
and Rose Hodges
&
Toby and Ian Spencer

# What's Inside

**Chapter 1:** Accidents Aren't Your Fault

**Chapter 2:** Why Accidents Happen

**Chapter 3:** Making Accidents STOP

**Chapter 4:** Staying Dry for Good

PLUS

A poop chart to hang in your bathroom!

You'll be dry soon!

I'm not a doctor, but I know all about poop and pee, too.

MY POOP CHART

1 — rabbit pellets

2 — big ol' logs

3 — thick and bumpy sausage

4 — smooth mushy snakes

5 — mushy blobs

6 — lumpy gravy

7 — diarrhea

## Hi, my name is Dr. Pooper.

Well, that's not my real name. But it's what my patients call me because I'm a pee and poop doctor. Really!

My job is to help kids who have accidents.

# Did you know millions of kids have accidents?

All over the world, kids have **pee** accidents at school, on the playground, and at home.

Many kids have **poop** accidents, too. Their poop falls out, and they don't even **feel** it.

Most of my **patients** wake up at night with wet **sheets**.

3

4

Sometimes adults wonder if kids have accidents on **purpose**. But kids don't, of course!

Accidents are a little like **sneezes**. You know how, when your nose gets tingly, you can't hold back that **ah-choo**?

# Same with accidents:
# They just happen – and fast!

But here's how accidents are **different** from sneezes: You can teach your body to make them **stop**.

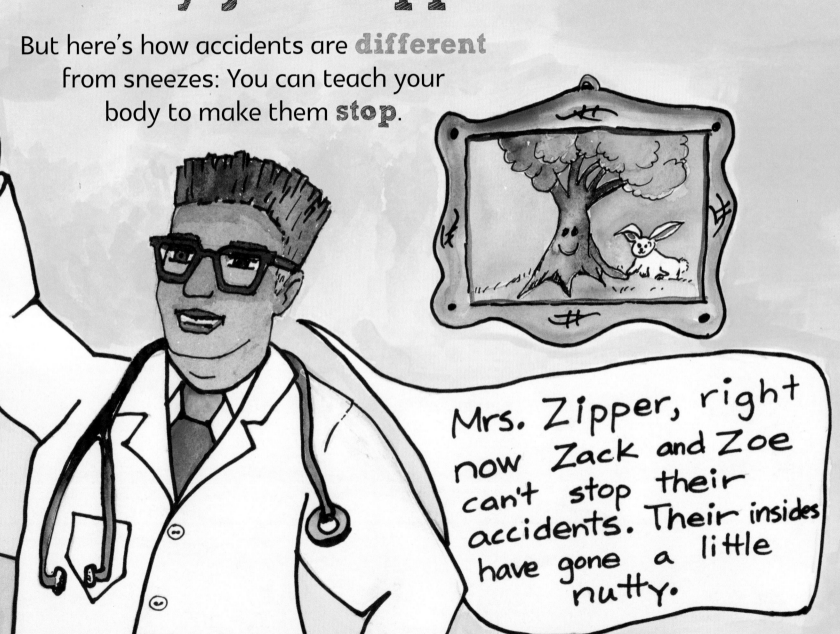

Mrs. Zipper, right now Zack and Zoe can't stop their accidents. Their insides have gone a little nutty.

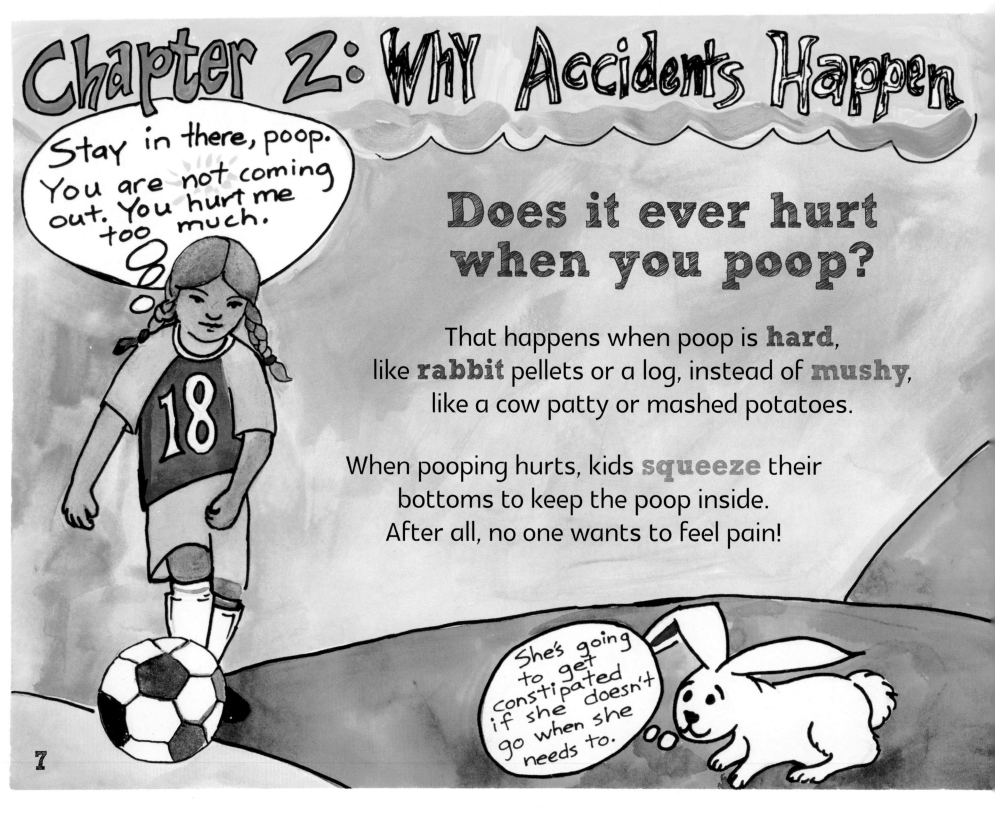

The poop pile-up happens in a stretchy tube called your **colon** — and especially at the end of your colon, called your **rectum**.

MOM! MY tummy hurts...

The **lump** gives some kids a stomachache.

Yum! Rat for lunch.

The poop pile hardens and **stretches** your colon, like a rat stretches a snake's belly.

When the lump gets big enough, **it squishes your bladder.**

The bladder is **stretchy**, like a balloon, and it has
a hole at the bottom where your pee comes out.

Imagine if you **squeezed** a water
balloon that had a tiny hole in it! The
water would **leak** out — like when you
have a pee accident or wet your bed.

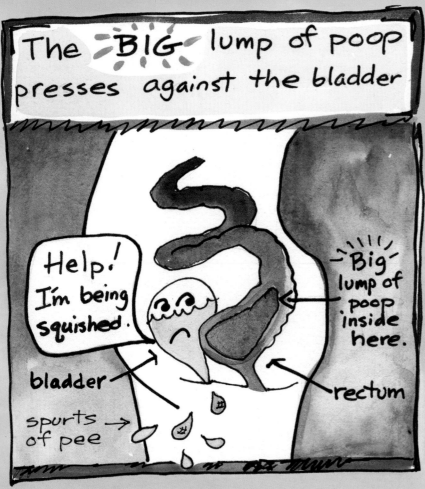

11

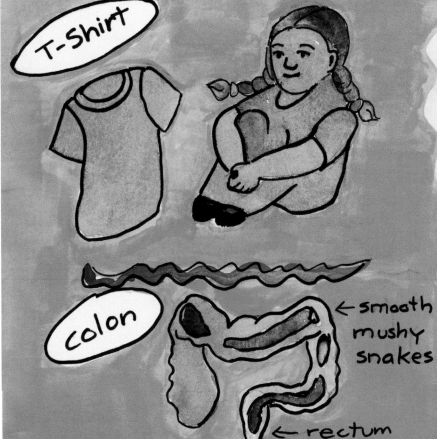

# How do poop accidents happen?

Well, that poop **lump** can stretch your colon so much that it becomes floppy, the way your shirt will get floppy if you **stretch** it over your knees.

A **floppy** colon can't keep in all your poop.
So, some of it just drops out your bottom.

Plus, when your **colon** is stretched, you can't always feel when poop needs to come out.
So, even more **piles** up.

14

Let's imagine a giant **hairball** is clogging your family's bathtub. Will that clog go away if you sit around and wait?

Waiting won't work. Time to call for help!

Zack, how long do you think we need to wait for the drain to unclog itself?

I don't know, Zoe. It sure is taking a long time.

Giant hairball in the bathtub plumbing

Of course not! You have to **clean** that hairball out of your pipe.

Same with your body: To make accidents **stop**, you have to clean that hard lump of poop out of your colon.

Then, your colon can **shrink** back to its normal size and stop squishing your bladder.

One way to clean out the lump is to **drink medicine that makes poop mushy.**

Then it will **plop** out of your bottom without hurting.

At first you'll need to drink **lots** of this **medicine**. You will be amazed at how much poop comes out.

You might poop **five** times in one day. Or even six!

But if your poop lump is **super** big
and hard, medicine might not work.

# You'll need an enema instead.

You'll take off your undies and lie on your side with your
knees bent. Mom or Dad will squirt water into your
bottom through a **small** tube.

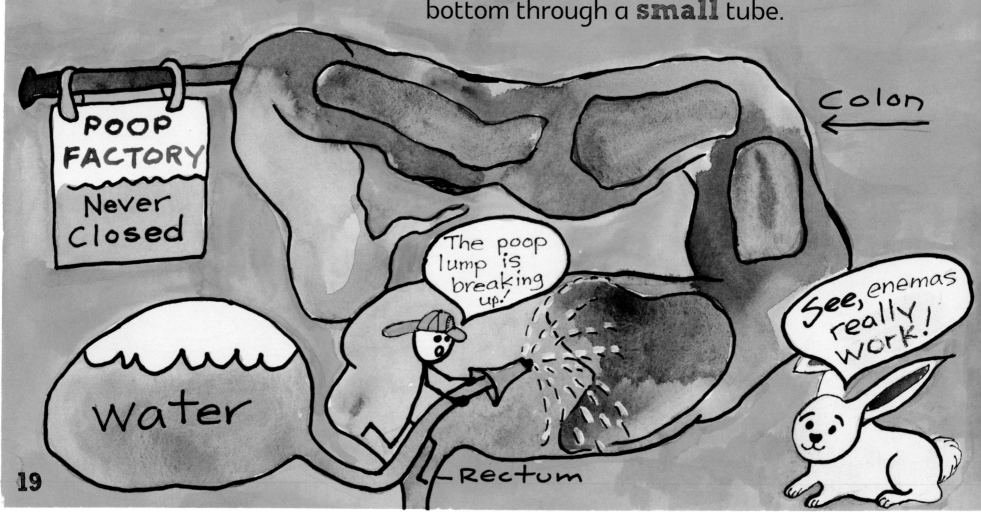

The **gentle** spray of water will loosen and **soften** the poop, the way water streaming from a hose can turn a **hard clump** of dirt into mud.

After a few minutes, you'll sit on the toilet. You will have a giant poop and feel so much **better**!

20.

# Yay! Your colon is unclogged!

Now, let's keep your poop **soft** so it doesn't get **stuck** again and pile up.

Medicine will help. So will drinking plenty of **water**, staying really **active**, and eating lots and lots of **fruits** and **vegetables**.

Some foods — like mac and cheese, chicken nuggets, and potato chips — will make your poop **hard**. So, don't eat foods like these often!

Stay super active.

22

# Also, keep pooping — a lot!

After **breakfast** and after **dinner**, sit on the toilet and give your poop a chance to come out.

Stay on the **toilet** for a full five minutes.

Read a book or play a game. Setting a **timer** can help, too.

24

Keeping your colon **clear** will definitely help you stay dry.

# But you have one other important job: peeing a lot.

If you pee **often**, your bladder will stay big and stretchy, and pee won't **leak** out.

If you hold your pee, your bladder will thicken and shrink. It might hiccup and spurt pee when you're not near a toilet.

# Don't cross your legs or squeeze your private area to keep pee inside!

When your **body** tells you it's time to pee, go to the bathroom — even if you are at **school**.

# One more thing!

Every time you poop, tell your mom or dad what your poop looks like.

If it looks hard, like rabbit **pellets**, a **log**, or a bumpy **sausage**, your colon is still clogged.

But if your poop looks like thin snakes or **mushy** blobs, you're all clear.

Hang this **poop chart** in your bathroom as a reminder!

# About the Authors

## Steve Hodges, M.D.

An associate professor of pediatric urology at Wake Forest University School of Medicine, Dr. Hodges specializes in children's toileting issues. He has authored numerous scientific journal articles and is co-author of *It's No Accident*. A goofball at heart, Dr. Hodges hopes *Accidents and Bedwetting Aren't Your Fault* will make kids smile, even laugh, about a topic that normally bums the heck out of them. Dr. Hodges lives in Winston-Salem, North Carolina, with his wife and three young daughters. He blogs at ItsNoAccident.net.

## Suzanne Schlosberg

Suzanne is a writer and editor known for her lighthearted take on health and parenting topics. She has written for Parents, Parenting, Shape, and numerous other media outlets. Her books include *The Good Neighbor Cookbook*, *The Ultimate Workout Log*, and *The Curse of the Singles Table*. Only when Suzanne collaborated with Steve Hodges on *It's No Accident* did she realize she'd taken the wrong approach to potty training her twin boys. Suzanne lives in Bend, Oregon. Her website is SuzanneSchlosberg.com.

# About the Artist

## Cristina Acosta

Cristina is a painter and designer known for her lyrical artistry and bold use of color. The author and illustrator of *Paint Happy* and illustrator of *When Woman Became the Sea*, Cristina has taught painting, drawing, and design. Cristina also designs home decor and contributes to interior-design magazines. Though Cristina's daughter is long past potty accidents, Cristina is excited to help children grow up confident and healthy. Cristina divides her time between Palm Springs, California, and Bend, Oregon. Her website is CristinaAcosta.com.

# The Story Behind the Story
## Information for Parents and Educators

### Q&A with Steve Hodges, M.D.

Associate professor of pediatric urology at Wake Forest University School of Medicine

Co-author of *It's No Accident*

*Bedwetting and Accidents Aren't Your Fault* is based on the approach to treating toileting troubles detailed in *It's No Accident: Breakthrough Solutions to Your Child's Wetting, Constipation, UTIs, and Other Potty Problems*. Here, Dr. Hodges explains the scientific foundation for his approach and answers questions he is commonly asked.

**Q: Aren't accidents a normal part of childhood?**

**A: That's a myth.** Accidents are common, but in potty-trained children, they almost always signal constipation and a bladder gone haywire. Children who never quite graduate to fully toilet trained or who continue to have accidents well after training typically aren't "late bloomers" or "rebellious"; they're constipated.

**Q: At what age should we take action if a child is wetting the bed?**

**A: I suggest age 4.** Bedwetting that seems "developmental" often can be fixed fairly easily, saving families from lost sleep, stress, and unnecessary expense. Don't wait until a child is 7! Though many children do outgrow bedwetting, others do not. I have many teenage patients whose bedwetting was dismissed for years.

**Q: How can you be sure bedwetting and accidents are caused by constipation?**

**A: The connection is confirmed daily in my practice and is well documented in the scientific literature.** The most rigorous studies were led by Sean O'Regan, M.D., a kidney specialist drawn to the topic because his 5-year-old son wet the bed. His son's rectum was so stretched by stool, tests showed, that the boy couldn't detect a tangerine-sized air balloon inflated in his bottom. Ultimately, Dr. O'Regan's research team tested hundreds of children with enuresis (pee accidents), encopresis (poop accidents), and recurrent urinary tract infections. Virtually all were stuffed with poop. After an enema regimen, their accidents and infections stopped. I discuss this research in *It's No Accident*.

Yum! Rat for lunch.

**Q: But don't some kids wet the bed because they are deep sleepers or have small bladders?**

**A:** Deep sleep may partly explain why a child with an overactive bladder doesn't wake up to pee, but it doesn't explain why the child's bladder is overactive to begin with. That reason is constipation. In my practice, virtually all children who wet the bed are shown by X-ray to be constipated. When their constipation is resolved, they stop wetting the bed — despite being "deep sleepers." Some kids do wet the bed because their bladders are small — but it's constipation, not a "late developing" bladder, that is compromising their bladder capacity.

**Q: Do you recommend medication to help resolve bedwetting?**

**A:** I don't. Medication can trick the kidneys into making less urine at night, but when the child stops taking the drug, the bedwetting typically returns. Medication doesn't fix the problem but rather covers it up.

**Q: How can I be sure a child is constipated?**

**A:** If the child is wetting the bed or having daytime pee or poop accidents, you can assume constipation is the problem. Other red flags: giant bowel movements, poops that resemble rabbit pellets or logs, recurrent UTIs, belly pain, the frequent or urgent need to pee, and pooping more than twice a day. Doctors who simply feel a child's abdomen and ask parents how often the child poops will miss most cases of constipation. An X-ray provides proof.

**Q: Isn't X-raying a child for constipation overkill?**

**A:** I don't think so. In our clinic we X-ray almost all children with wetting issues. About 90 percent are severely constipated, though only 5 percent of their parents had an inkling. Most of these children were referred by pediatricians who also missed the rectal clogs. The radiation dose of an abdominal X-ray is the same dose you get from simply living for three months. The amount of good you can do for a child by accurately diagnosing constipation far outweighs the risks of a couple of plain X-rays.

**Q: Which is more effective: laxatives or enemas?**

**A:** Enemas! Often PEG 3360 (the generic name for MiraLAX) will make poop soft but fail to fully clean out the rectum. Many parents assume their child will refuse enemas. But in my experience, when you explain enemas are the ticket to dryness, the child is plenty willing to give them a try.

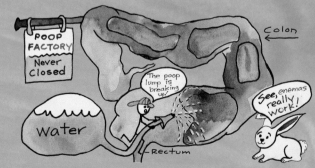

You can find much more information about bedwetting and accidents at ItsNoAccident.net and in *It's No Accident*.

# Acknowledgments

We are immeasurably grateful to artist Cristina Acosta, whose clever and upbeat illustrations brought our ideas to life in vivid color. Brilliant!

Thank you all so much!

Our hardworking and talented graphic designer, Dyan Roth, did a beautiful job, as always. And our excellent photographer, Gary Alvis, worked at the speed of light. Thank you, Nancy Kruh, for reviewing the book with a fine-tooth comb.

So many families contributed to this book without knowing it, simply by sharing their stories with us and asking wise questions. Insights from Kathy Steinert and Angela Villalobos led directly to certain illustrations, as did ideas from Ian and Toby Spencer.

On a more fundamental level, we are grateful to Dr. Sean O'Regan, whose impeccable studies provide the scientific foundation to the concepts explained in this book and in *It's No Accident*.

## Praise for Bedwetting and Accidents Aren't Your Fault

"Every family dealing with accidents or bedwetting should own this engaging and eye-opening book!"

– Amy McCready, founder of Positive Parenting Solutions
and author of *If I Have to Tell You One More Time…*

"I'm thrilled by this caring, empathetic approach to toileting difficulties."

– Marc A. Levitt, M.D., Surgical Director, Center for Colorectal and Pelvic Reconstruction Pediatric Surgery, Nationwide Children's Hospital, Columbus, Ohio

"This creative and inspirational book will give children confidence."

– Bob Sears, M.D., pediatrician and co-author of the *The Baby Book*

"This book will make kids laugh — and make parents grateful for solutions that work."

– Heather Wittenberg, Psy.D., author of *Let's Get This Potty Started!*

## Praise for It's No Accident

"This terrific book will help parents better advocate for their kids. I am grateful to have this great resource to recommend to families."

– Shelly Vaziri Flais, M.D., pediatrician,
co-editor of *The Big Book of Symptoms* and author of *Raising Twins*

"*It's No Accident* has completely changed my approach to treating children with urinary issues. I find it very rewarding to actually be able to help a lot of these kids now."

– Daniell Rackley, M.D., pediatric urologist,
Southeastern Urological Center, Tallahassee

"Reading *It's No Accident* was a lightbulb moment for me. We used Dr. Hodges' approach with my son, and it worked!"

– Sally Kuzemchak, M.S., R.D., nutritionist and
blogger at realmomnutrition.com